T0090360

The Written Word

POETRY AND THOUGHTS

By

Dr. Lisa Ladin-Bramet

Order this book online at www.trafford.com
or email orders@trafford.com

Most Trafford titles are also available at major online book retailers.

Printed in the United States of America.

ISBN: 978-1-4269-4888-6 (sc)
ISBN: 978-1-4269-4889-3 (e)

Library of Congress Control Number: 2010918398

Trafford rev. 01/27/2011

 www.trafford.com

North America & international
toll-free: 1 888 232 4444 (USA & Canada)
phone: 250 383 6864 ♦ fax: 812 355 4082

Table of Contents

The Written Word

April 17 1980

Writing is an action
That lets my thoughts come through
Yet when my thoughts are written
Some answers come to view

Armed with pen and paper
I let myself go free
The flow of ink runs wild
Expressed emotionally

At times I write in pleasure
Sometimes I write in pain
No matter what my reason is
I write thoughts just the same

Most writers write for others
And publish work with pride
Though many writers write for fun
Most write to see inside

When writers are discovered
They know not what's to come
For critics travel far and wide
To comment, shine and shun

I've often thought of writing
For all the world to see
However I find poetry
I've written just for me

Should someone ask me nicely?
To share my work in print
I'd have to think it over
And write my thoughts content

Valentine's Day

January 14 1980
Revised February 20 1980

The day of hearts
And what of mine
Perhaps amidst a wonderland
With tenderness of hidden parts

Ere my dream could come to view
New perspectives dodge my touch
But pass me by so easily seen
Once again love comes anew

The eve has come of romance
Found Eros bound at play
Teasing all who faired his smile
Wedged with heart amidst his glance

All who once were struck?
Held sights of visions passed
Searching for the unfound dream
Against the weight of cupid's luck

Where do I venture the missing souls?
Departing once again in life
Thinking thankless thoughts to be
Their self fulfilling goals

Perhaps 'tis true of death
Wherein we see no light
The peace of which we search through love
Denies our very breath

The thought remains to be
Our memories' eternal birth
An end must come to written words
For days of heart to grieve

Alliterative Analysis

February 22 1980

Poetic prose poses a prayer
For fairest friends fondly free
My magic mind moody men
Who heartlessly hear her hymns?

Vastly vague voice vacancy
Shallow shores shower speech
Barren borders break but bear
Gallant girl gently glance

Truth tells tales to taunt then tease
Lovers learn lustfully leave
Caring can't command clear court
Desirous dates do dwell dead dreams

This poem delivers prayer
For friends and lovers free
My charm does touch these men of moods
Who know not what I mean

The emptiness of words
As spoken through the air
Are hardly heard as said
Tho women know thru stares

Truth is pain when left unknown
Lovers use their lust to grow
The caring that they share when close
Annihilate their time alone

The Search

March 6 1980

Love comes and goes in many forms
Often I know not the shape
Explore I must, my heart to warm
Though inner sense misleads the rape

How hard I search for one to share
The day's events, the thoughts I bear
For every time I meet a match
A moment's glimpse is all I catch

For years I shared myself with Russ
Though he knows not his destiny
The distance parting both of us
Has helped me grow internally

Why do I search for one to share?
The day's events, the thought I bear
And why each time I meet a match
A moment's glimpse is all I catch

The pain I feel in each release
Causes me to back away
Rebuilding walls that taunt and tease
The men who try to share my days

I realize my need to share
The day's events, the thought I bear
Is based upon my need to match
With one of whom my love can catch

March 18 1980

I believe I know not
True consequences of my actions
I believe I'm shown not
Validity of point
I believe I care not
To live with lies
I believe that understanding
Must come mutually
How are we to know
How each judge's trust
Must we search thru
Experience
To know the consequences
Of our actions?
Can we not overcome
The end
Before venturing
Upon the journey
I'm not responsible

For anyone else's ignorance
But I must face
My own naïveté
I'll pay the price for words
Meant not to be said
But I cannot be held
Liable for thoughts in other heads
All must be said aloud
Should the form displease
Then excuse me
For I meant not my words to
Express the essence
Of my feelings.
As understood by all
Who hear my voice

Sadness

October 24 1971

Happiness has left and gone
The smile that once was there,
And now a frown was just put on
Now sadness fills the air.

Something happened which I know
Has left its pains inside,
The atmosphere is now quite cold
We've been taken on a ride.

The View from which we all can see
Is dark and gloomy, cold & grey,
Nothing pleasant could it be
The sadness ride aches all the way.

What gets you on this awful ride?
Unpleasant all the way,
The happiness has left inside
Sympathetic people say.

Don't let sadness change your style
It hurts you time again,
Lift your spirits laugh awhile
In due time it will mend.

Untitled

How can this child wander
Alone
With the world in his
Way
Like a wall built of
Stone
And how can this child
Give love to a song
When the notes are avoiding
The music they long
And why does this child
Enclose all the pain
In a heart that has suffered
Time and again
Perhaps the reason
Lies in a soul
That has opened the doors
Of an empty hole
Only to answer
The promise of........

Untitled

I know how hard it is to care
To worry when the room is bare
To hurt the one you know you love
By caring more in tightened glove
Yet you should know I'm only human
Loving life the best I can
Mistakes are meant to be I guess
And made to show the loving best
So please forgive me try I will
To be a better person still
But if I happen to go astray
Please lead me back the right way
Forget the bitterness you've shed
Unlock the anger inside your head
I guess I've failed your honor test
No more chances I agree
Will make me right again I see

Childs Play

"Who is she?" they say as she stands by the rail
She answers unspoken through whispering winds
They glide through the water center a raft
Splashing contentedly carefree 'til eight
Asking if per chance it might rain
Whisked away as the summer sets a day
Wondering why I sit here awaiting him
Can they be wanting my attention oh I see
A cut on the foot in need of some care
Sure I'll check for a band aid upstairs
They looked at the bongs, the bottles and such
Draping their eyes and avoiding to tamper
I cleaned off the blood cautious of pain
Explored the wound under the lamp again
Taped gauze to protect her and quietly gazed
Following down to continue this prose
As the young ones departed in humble relief
Thanking my help 'tho I'd not said a word
It was nice to know I could help someway
Still the night beckons forth and above
And there's still no sign of the one I know
Like the storm that approaches these skies
Thunder within can materialize or fade clear
And I shall not be around if the stars
Should dance the galaxy in delight
Meeting in May if he cares to relate
I've sat quite awhile and he's bringing me down

Untitled

When a man decides to enter
In a sense he is part of your life
No matter how close he hits center
The woman need not act as wife
A lover is hard to entangle
For barriers must tumble down
The closeness can otherwise mangle
All personal space each has found
When a man wants to witness all actions
A woman has nowhere to hide
And in witnessing every reaction
The man can see right up inside
Now a woman can easily master
The art of deceiving a man
If man is persistently after control
Then a woman is damned
True a woman can close off her senses
Pretending her feelings are lost
It may sound as if woman is fragile
You may choose to believe she is weak
Yet if cornered by man she is agile
And her truth can be vulgar in peak
If you wonder why this has been written
It's because of a man who has dared
To open this woman and drift on
The feelings of which she is scared

Untitled

Windy days in dreaming dire
Kindle bright internal fire
Sweetly glaze my path of sight
My wings shall beckon wind in flight

Tarry not the journey thus
For want has need of all in us
Deliver souls in parting ways
Keep not the knowledge midst the daze

Parting sorrow bends the willow
Floating currents mark the bough
I do beseech the weeping tree
To dance the heart of soul for me

Shattered clouds disperse their path
Allowing wind to show its wrath
For humans know not wind in force
Though mankind hastens from its course

Quirkier sunlight braze the sky
The wind will sing your lullaby
And nature thus will glide in time
Releasing all in powered prime

Shallow waters flow the bed
Of rivers laden well with lead
The tarnished forests cry with shame
For man has rendered forests lame

Thoughts...

Freedom abused can result in temporary incarceration to allow one time to think of the blessings of freedom.

I can sense the pain he feels being locked in a cage like an animal. However, he claims to have overpaid his price for his crime. Who is to be the judge of punishment? The criminal? No. The criminal cannot truly know when he has paid the price for his actions for such knowledge is inherent only when he has a second chance to commit the same crime.

How does one know the truth from lies? When the truth is spoken, the flow of words is painless and smooth, the heart is free from burden, and the mind is calm with peace. But a lie carries with it weight, pain and disunity all of which are visible to any who can view clearly and objectively.

Windless days bear the melody of chimes.

Passengers are the carriers of travel from rear view windows. Drivers are the directors of travel who have no access to viewing the journey.

Sickness is health disguised. Health is nudity of self.

The Day after
St. Valentine's Day and the Gift

Stopped my tears from endless streams
Held the package tight
Could not bear to break a seal
Tried to call just three short rings
Held your presence in my mind
Heard my heart rejoice with love
Thought you were beside me then
Knew your smile had touched me kind
Heard my phone though unaware
Reached to hear the call
Finally knew who it was
Knew I did not care
Said my words so distantly
Had to raise my voice
Heard him say, "It's been a while"
Glimpsed at his uncertainty
Caringly ignored him well
Didn't feel ashamed
Saw my world with clarity
Meant my love had left its spell
Slowly opened up the gift
Shed my heart to you
Wanted just to hold you tight
Puckered sweet and swift
Know I'll love you in a way
The world will want to hear
Our blossomed growth this cherished life
Every breath we say

January 28

There's a reason for my not sleeping
Yes a reason for writing so late
If I knew why hunger came creeping
I'd have eaten all I could take
Though I'm tired I find myself writing
Yes I'm smoking a cigarette too
Though tomorrow will come quick as lightening
There's no alternate path to pursue
I wonder why I am with energy
'Tween my school and my work I'm fulfilled
Perhaps I have thoughts unintentionally
That I need to resolve while I'm stilled
I feel ready to try to return again
To the dreams I have yet to relieve
I am sure that this pause I capture in pen
Will lead to the answers I weave

November 17 1979

My Irishman blue eyed gent
My blond haired Irishman
Our time was so well spent
Soft spoken words I hardly heard
Pursuer of kindness to all in reach
I could never equate my love in word
My Irishman speaker of truth
Lover of softness, gentle touch
Bearer of songs, wisdom and youth
My blond haired Irishman
Where shall you go?
Perchance to pass my life again
Our time was so well spent
Together we shared so honestly
Our moods nay we e're repent
My Irishman you are my friend
My heart does share your soul
For love like ours must transcend
All the boundaries in this life
Yes Irishman we married
But not as man and wife
Dear Irishman my blue eyed gent
Fair thee well this day
To you I send my compliment
Such verse could ne're display

November 27

And on this rainy day mid week
A woman tried but could not sleep
Her friend knew not if she was well
The child she bore would die – pray tell
To whom would words of comfort reach
And who's to say just why it rained
Perhaps a lesson love doth teach
By broken dreams that lie in pain
The babe is harmlessly withheld
For life as such cannot exist
Before the noontime hour fell
The dawn of death would come betwixt
Who's to say what job would come
If life were easier said than done
Perhaps the child, the soul within
Twas meant a life to not begin
The karma is done this very day
And mother of child a price will pay
Father will wonder forever to know
Whether this day will cease to grow

* * * * * * *

Prayer

Blessed be life, unknown without death
Light come upon us this moment in time
Where there be comfort silently layeth
Thy heart of peace within this rhyme

Jan. 23 1980:
Memorial for the
State of the Union Address

The moments pass by, and I gaze through glass
To watch the traffic of an aging sky
The peace we revere as a nation will pass
A war creeps upon us, this decade does sigh
Our president warned that the Russians prepare
For should they decide to meet our decree
United Americans gather to dare
The soviet strength they wish us to see
My friends are of age to fight in this war
Though we have beseeched our world to rest
The turmoil beckons the pride of our core
And bloodshed will tarnish the soil in test
My lover is sentenced to fight for our cause
Perchance if we gather the women as well
I'll know not if ever our love will face laws
To bind our devotion this life which we dwell
I fear not the end of this worldly mirage

The beliefs I contain are not bound by my body
However I know now my feelings are lodged
'Tween desires of flesh, still seeds in the pod
I've mentioned my visions of war in my prime
I wished I could carry a child in my womb
Should war take the world apart in time?
The birth I desire will not leave its tomb
Generations I've grown with do protest for peace
We see no just cause in destruction of life
Our wishes of heart, ne're will they cease
Yet we have no control over worldly strife
A prayer will be said by young people now
Who fear for the life they've grown to live
With each passing word, in silence we vow
That in order to take, we must always give

Sam

Through waves I rush to meet your gaze
Though I can see the pain in your eyes
Tell me why can I not clear my heart
Without suction of the air I breathe
Sway along the side of a hill
Show me the way through the mesh
Unleash the smiles from your soul
I shall not go beyond the 'bow
Nor cast a shadow upon the castle
Amidst sands of your dreams
Climb the skies along the webs of night
Changes follow suit if the way is clear
Hear me sail for floods shall weep
In half mast pretense of sympathy
My love is patterned bright in awe
Life within in harmony on your day
Sleep tight too sweet in flight…fall
Catch you I will for you belong
To my consciousness for all its worth
Do not part I shall not bear
Yes my dear 'tis true I care
And in all my will I shall be there
For you, for always, for love
Swept in song I make my place
For the poet has truly released
Feelings for a day – your day
A celebration in birth of creativity
Love,
Lisa

Strong Minded Workers

June 2

I'm a lady of mind with a will of my own
I work in a world where a mind has no say
Where work is dependent on games people play
And the rules favor only technicians who stay

I'm a lady of mind with pride in myself
I work in an office where men rule in vain
Where kissing an ass is the best way to gain
Where a strong minded worker is only a pain

Just why do these trippers of power control
These technical robots who haven't a soul
Demanding allegiance for wages in pay
And the strong minded workers have too much to say
Yes the strong minded workers must suffer or pay

I'm a lady whose talent deserves to be shared
I work with three men who are angry with me
Cause I won't bleed and die for sycophancy
No I won't live my life for this damn company

I'm a lady, an artist who strives in her field
I work hard to upgrade each product I see
But I won't let technicians decide life for me
They can't decide life on their own can't you see?

Just where do these trippers of power control
These technical robots who haven't a soul
Demanding allegiance for wages in pay
These trippers of power control every play
Yes the strong minded workers must suffer this way

I'm a lady whose eyes have seen workers lose faith
I work with employees who've lost guts inside
They value their paychecks much more than their pride
And the money they worship the trippers divide

So how can we stop the trippers' control?
These technical robots who haven't a soul
Deny them allegiance for wages in pay
Refuse to pay homage to games that they play
Be strong minded workers in every which way

Silence

October 20 1971

Quietness silently proud
Something that can't be heard aloud
Nothing coming from a crowd
The society of words.

A peacefulness within itself
A voice that shouts aloud
The sound of tiny, little elves
The noise made from a cloud

A mouse's personality
A teacher's prayer to God
Is gained in popularity
A silent little nod

Something rarely exchanged among
A friend or someone near
A sound that's always been around
A sound that you should hear

Something needed in the land
Never before heard
Listen to its soft command
And think about its words

Childhood

January 24 1972

Childhood comes once so dear
To visualize fantasies so clear
Acting the parts of those so near
Moods of triumph, bravery and fear.

Playing with the future and unafraid
Thinking not as time parades
Wondering when it all will fade
The lives of those whom you have made.

Maturing slowly as you grow
Managing a life you control
Copying elders from below
Never quitting from the show.

Education soon takes rule
Up at 8 and off to school
Addressed as student or pupil
Seeing those who are kind or cruel.

The world is bigger than you thought
Everything is sold or bought
Doing things you should have not
Punishment when you are caught.

Experience is what you've learned
Grown up now, your life has turned
Stages of life, where you've returned
Here or there you have been burned.

What becomes of this life?
Difficult and full of strife
Your hearts been cut as well as sliced
The good and bad denotes the price

The Cemetery

Wandering through the city of death
Upon entering a sign of life
Gazing at those who have entered tombs
People scattered hands apart
Realizing respect at cause
Imagination lives about
Eternal rest upon the soul
A field of those who've stopped to rest
Unhappiness through the atmosphere
Flowers gifts of those who share
Lives to heaven some to hell
Solitude between the walls
Ground dug up to lie within
Those departing from this world
Men & women equal alike
A shadow has befallen them

Time

Time pauses for those who keep pace,
Yet it feels for those who are slower.
Eternity is the essence of time.
Those deserving have not wasted.
People concentrate on their one life,
But try to rush as to fill up the day.
And what is accomplished then?
Favor is not it times vision,
Death has never entered time
Nor has it disturbed the walls thereof.
Time's castle stands erect and strong,
Never to be destroyed… as long as time exists.

* * * * * * *

Friendship

Someone precious ever so few
Is there when needed without a cue
Understanding without a doubt
Kindness within as well as throughout

Fun to be with anywhere
Willing to listen, ready to care
A person you cannot pawn
Compassionate from eve to dawn

An agreement between the two
A bond between me and you
Nothing perfect but just the same
When it is broken one feels lame

Together

A piece of mind, so desired
Love that is real and pure
The heart, as deeply fired
A remedy or cure
Passion filling the hopes
Sharing a feeling of content
The soul over slopes
A message after being sent
Creating visions of ecstasy
Impossible to part
Clearly and explicitly
Love filling the heart

* * * * * * *

The Desert

As the wind bursts across the plains
Sand drifting through periods of time
Nighttime as the day refrains
Endless soil against its prime
Mountains closing forth the day
Animals surround the hills
Lifetime in the desert's way
Has its sorrows and its thrills

"Five Ways to Balanced Intelligence"

There are six ways of asking a question.
Only one type can lead you to grief.
If you use this one way I can promise,
The answers will yield no relief.

"WHO" will give answers on people.
"WHEN" will give answers on time.
"WHERE" will direct you to places.
"WHAT" is the subject in mind.
Are you ready to hear out the crime?
Listen my friends as I caution you now,
For this question works well in sublime.

If you want to bring on the defenses,
Or justify someone's to blame.
The use of this word leads to wrong or right,
And to mind a most negative frame.

Example:
"Why were you late for your meeting?"
"Because someone called me you see."
(Is the answer accepted? No. Here comes the WHY.
To place blame, in this typical scene.)

"Why are you always so sad dear?"
"Just because, it is not your concern."
(The person who asked has been cornered, oh no.
Now defenses will come in return.)

The question of WHY is quite useless.
Working only with cause and effect.
The further one uses this resource,
Is the limit one has for respect.

If you feel you can judge someone's actions.
Or feel you can tell RIGHT from WRONG.
Your importance of self is larger than life.
In whose KINGDOM do you now belong?

Or perhaps you are wearing your armor.
Are you feeling quite low to the ground?
Does GUILT overflow the world that you see?
Yes? The meaning of life has no sound.

Is either direction worthwhile?
Must answers yield reasons to join?
Both CAUSE and EFFECT are two sides in one.
'Tis best to just throw out the coin.

For either direction will BLAME or DEFEND.
Neither informs without sides.
To balance the space with thoughts not stance,
Requires intelligent strides.

Example:
"In what respect are you sad dear?"
"I am sad when I think of our fights."
"How can you avoid being tardy?"
"Perhaps holding calls on those nights."

Have the questions been answered my friends?
Are there positive means to reply?
Can you see the respect given both ways?
When you use other questions save WHY?

Can you see how these questions leave options?
Can you see what options can do?
Can you see when answers are open?
Where freedom will widen your view?

Now let us begin to use these five means,
To gather the knowledge we crave.
And if someone belabors to ask you just WHY?
The absurd will lead them astray.

Example:
"Why did you say that to me?"
"So that polar bears can wear their garter belts in the spring."

As the Wind Carries Me

In your eyes I can hear
The wind laughing
Through your smile I can feel
The suns touch
With your heart comes the
Waves of freedom I seek
Of life in my dreams
And such
That the wind speaks to me
In this moment we meet
Of warmth in the sun of
My soul
So I search for the feelings
So few can share
When we meet the layers
Unfold
Then I hear the wind laughing
Inside us
I feel the suns touch
In our smile
The waves of freedom
Are discovered in heart
And my dreams live
Life for awhile

Untitled

How long it seems
Since time before I sat
In the circle with the wind
Writing freely of things

How fresh it seems
To feel the wind on my neck
And a chill down my spine
Harmonious words I dream

How still it seems
To hear the ambience of life
View the dance of the trees
Sensing cold through my jeans

How it is just today
Tomorrow of yesterday's change
A balance of being I guess
The division of sensory traits

Untitled

I saw you turn away from me
Then close your heart
Showing all the hurt you feel
Telling me my kiss is like an open wound
That scars the sore it tries to heal

I can't hide the shame inside
For the hurt I wear to clothe my skin
How can I express my love to you
When the pain confuses me again

Are we listening to our sense of hardship
Will we find the strength to carry on
Can we bear the weight of fear
Must it crush the sense that we belong

The nightmares come to haunt you
With a loneliness
Of worries feeding on your mind
You're telling me the isolation must exist
To push the selfishness behind

I can't hide the need within
To find the self that I have locked away
Must I change the path I take
When the words are searching out to blame

Untitled

He walks alone
Trusting no one by his side
All the people he meets
Have a secret they all hide
His moves are swift
With a glancing sweep he kills
As the voices of love
Brush a heart that renders chills
He's a loner
Eyes of steel that melt away
In anger
His fears are at bay
He's mindful
Of the souls that cross his stride
With vengeance
The past is retried
He waits for death
Like a man awaits a bride
The passion he feels
Severs all who stand aside
He dreams of days
When his gun is laid to rest

Only time will tell
If the trust will pass his test
He's a sinner
His faith in God is weak
All the prayers at night
Were just words his mouth would speak
He's an angel
Serving justice for the crimes
That haunt him
Like incessant chimes
His thoughts are pain
Executed with great pride
Though there's much to gain
Laying all the hurt aside
He's beset with strength
Like a thunderstorm at night
And he'll go the length
In this struggle for the light

The Path in the Darkness

October 18 1993

1. The voice is distant, moving father away
3. To a place out of touch from those who care
5. Yet each bridge that is built to lend a path
6. Lies dormant of use, avoided with wrath
4. The builder accused of endangered despair
2. As the heart wanders searching in disarray

1. Where are you going when love comes to call
3. The pain offers guidance to service the fear
5. Whose voice whispers truth in shadows of mind
6. Is the presence you seek supportive in kind?
4. Are the thoughts befriending the anguish you hear
2. Perhaps the allegiance means nothing at all

1. Can you feel the arms that reach to your soul
3. Rejected by anger, grieving the loss
5. Abandoned in service of union and peace
6. Searching forgiveness to honor release
4. At a price growing higher each day in cost
2. This lover awaits the half to be whole

1. Sweet angel of mercy descend to him now
3. He searches through darkness, looking for light
5. Hearing the voices that echo deceit
6. Hopeful this journey will end in retreat
4. I wait for his footsteps well into the night
2. For the presence his quest attempts to endow

With prayers I succumb to the will
Of one who has parted and
Returns not still

Untitled

On a dark night
In the hills not far away
The glowing eyes lend sight
To all the wildlife who hear
A distant hum
Signals to the birds in flight
The hunter travels soon
To end the days of some whose might
Cannot carry them to safety
Though the wilderness
Is a hallowed ground
Man emerges boldly
Buying all he's found
Raping nature's home
Without care or woe
'Till the earth is swept to dust
Her voice withholding sound
Weeping for the shadows
Cast by stars
Bathed by the moon
The spirit wanders in search
Of those who once knew
Why it all began

January 19 1996

Injustice occurs many times in our lives
We ask God for answers and hear no replies.
Often I wonder if answers exist,
To the questions we ask as our pain persists.

Why do some live when others must die?
Who makes the choice if there's will to survive?
Can we determine the path of our fate?
Or is our demise a vision comes late?

I continue to question the nature of being;
Though many have told me it's all in believing.
The fact of the matter rests in this thought:
If God is just then why is life not?

Untitled

A friend had come into my life
Or so I heard him say
For friendship was the term he used
To measure loves display

I winced when I first heard this term
From thoughts of other men
Yet he insisted I discern
That lovers often end

As days passed by, within his touch
The term arose with peace
I found myself in love as such
And felt my heart release

To trust this friend I questioned not
Nor did I search my dreams
For every spoken word he sought
With openness it seems

The feelings grew beyond my will
Revealing thoughts inside
I flourished in his arms and still
A caution did reside

I knew not what had troubled me
Though pictures came to view
The cards had shown what I could see
Such visions I withdrew

It came to pass amidst the night
This fear I would not place
When I was yielded clear in sight
The answer face to face

I'd asked of him but one request
To honor what we shared
For should another wish to rest
And if he truly cared

That he would tell me with respect
Before the moment passed
To give me choice should I elect
Withdrawing love amassed

Her words did pierce my heart with tears
I asked him to reply
As moments wakened all my fears
His words did not deny

Now hours slowly move in time
His presence but a dream
I know not what I share in rhyme
Save hurt and pain I deem

And yet I wait to hear his voice
To know this heart that lied
For from his thoughts I'll make a choice
That burns and taunts my pride

I cannot say I'd do the same
For I was in his bind
Perhaps the fear of loss remains
Demanding us to find

That honesty in friends is rare
Unless we chance our fears
For if we say we truly care
Then we must risk our tears

If only he would come to test
He'd know I judge him not
Yet I will make the same request
I love this man a lot

Should he not honor me again
I shall release my love
But I believe he is my friend
That we will rise above

I ask in prose for his reply
For time is walking slow
These words appear to pacify
What I feel and truly know

For Patsy

June 10 1990

Though I know you not well
I have come to respect
Your guidance at school
And the tasks you direct

The patience you share
With all ages at heart
Is coupled with care
In whole and in part

You are known for eyes
That observes every sign
For thoughts that are wise
And for paths you align

For wisdom and knowledge
To counsel or advise
Be it thoughts of college
Or emotions that rise

As your path is at change
And this portion at end
May I share this exchange
Of value as assistant and friend

I bid you contentment
In all that you do
Know by my statements
I too will miss you

Untitled

The fairytale of images whose opulence it seems,
Rests along the roadside, parked by make-believe
Who's to say this house of gold will shelter our decay
For all who enter in this dream, awake in disarray.

Perhaps this treasure's beauty appears within our reach
For many statements tied to chrome insist that 'life's a beach'
Yet aspirations rise above to mingle with the clouds
And all the rays of starlight shine on different crowds.

Landscaped in decorum that hides the dream from view
Are roads that lead to nowhere and souls who rush right through
The formless ride deliveries as token signs of care
Alongside men of beauty who notice when you stare

Where are hearts to wander when gazing past the gates
That lead into a wonderland with claims of higher stakes.
Perhaps we've built this mirror of the heaven that we need
In order to substantiate the level of our greed

Still many shall in quiet awe approach these walls of fame
Enchanted by the interplay of all there is to gain
In polished stance with deference they search to find a place
Where they remain within the reach of those who need a face

And still the years pass quietly as aging takes its course
The pretty boys and girls mature as young ones come on board
As cyclical as night and day the story turns again
To pages filled with chances passed by those 'who knew a friend'.

I walk along the silent lot past cars of every make
Waving to a lonely guard who's posted at a 'Take'
Humbled by the brilliance that shines behind each door
Yet knowing that I've touched this force many years before

The struggle to reveal oneself to geniuses at play
Is tougher than the heartbreak that locks this dream away
But now that I have seen the game and played a minor role
I recognize that this dream lacks the essence of my soul.

Untitled

When beauty comes to paradise
Birds tend the air in flight
Gliding on the whisper wind
As boats are passing by
Voices from the water tell
Of passing dreams by night

* * * * * * *

In Response

February 22 1990

A poem came to me one eve
With words to touch my heart
Amidst the lines I did perceive
The poet's soul in part

Though I knew not his purpose
I sensed his words as truth
And while I read, I felt his search, as
Eyes of one in youth

Beseeching me for answers
My words could not be found
'Midst visions of two dancers
Whose touch was all but sound

My body ached in silence
Each breath I held at bay
To ponder my reliance
Of thoughts I chose to say

It mattered not what words were said
For he could read me well
He knew the thoughts within my head
Were charmed and cast in spell

My answer to the song in rhyme
He held within his touch
And as this poet captures time
She shares her thoughts as such

February 18 1984

I want to write a poem to you
One you'll read with heart
To tell you all the thoughts I knew
Have pulled us both apart

You've asked me where the ideas came
For whom I live my ways
I wanted you to share the blame
To feel my pain in days

The cries that came from deep within
Tried hard to plead release
You mirrored every move again
I looked whenever I'd please

Soon your mood – your pain came clear
You bore the dirt beyond the need
Silence curbed my sight, my dear
And then I saw my seed

The limbs now grow quite rigid
Their shape was formed in vain
For what reward to limit
A love quite free of name

Apologies are raining skies
That disappears to mist
Just where are you to hide the lies
The promises of jist?

The room within had closed its door
To rest in peace from love deformed
And then to hear I loved you more
Awakened caution justly born

The gaiety and laughter heard
In days when we first met
Were natural not just in word
From the woman, not the debt

The price she paid so willingly
For goods she did not want
Disposed awareness instantly
In dreams her days did haunt

She looked to see her face one day
Her mother came to view
And then she looked inside to say
"I'm returning this to you"

His prayers were answered just in time
But why live every moment
Hanged for what? For no one's crime
You say that there's no comment?

And why did she renig the love
She cherished naturally?

To pay a price for goods unsold
Yet bought as sanity?

Yes I need to write a poem to you
I need to show my love....

February 13 1984

Don't play the game for me my love
The house and the kids don't exist
If you're helpless to make any changes
Don't play the game for me.

Don't go insane for me my love
The humanness comes from within
If you're helpless to make any changes
Don't go insane for me.

Do be yourself for you my love
See what's inside and reach with your heart
If I'm helpless to make any changes
Do be yourself for you.

Do live your life, be aware my love
Reach out to the few who are real
If I'm helpless to make changes now
Do live your life be aware.

As I write what I hear and see my love
The woman you love feels your pain
We're both not helpless to make any changes
So what are we doing again?

April 2 1984

I look into your eyes, winter's come to pass

The snow has turned to ice

The doors seem frozen shut

I feel the chilling wind creep up by back

And my tears are but the rain that follows next

In the latent months of winter, spring must come

Can the hope be but a moment's breath in time

Is this winter here to stay

Will it conquer the sunshine

If I close my eyes and dream again

Will winter end

Now I know the sun is precious

Will it come again

Can denial be forgiven if it's lived in vain

When a nightmare wakes the dreams

Will the dreams remain?

Can I conquer hope awaken life

When spring is near

Does the winter of a heart in pain

Believe in fear

If belief is all I cherish
Why must pain take weight
Can I balance what was once believed
As destined fate
Yes this dreamer sees the nightmare
Of a winter storm
Yes this dreamer wakes amidst the storm
The nightmares live
And she sees the warmth exists when she
Knows how to give
Let me reach into your eyes and help
This winter pass
Can we meet the snow together
Can I thaw the ice
Can I open up the doors again
Can I block the wind
Can I dry away our tears
Let the warmth begin
If I am indeed a nightmare
Let the dream believe again
Let me in or let this nightmare end

Untitled

Though darkness comes by day this time
I search for meaning through this rhyme
Traversing worlds that shield from view
The inner self I thought I knew

To travel far away from home
Calls up the fears I have alone
Reveals the love I know by heart
The love my fear attempts to part

Selfishness beguiles this mind
To travel roads outside of time
For in each step I will find out
The answers I have cried about

Could I handle time away
From one I love I could not say
For when I had my option here
The pain was hidden by my fear

I run from all I love in life
From being chained to every strife
Bonded by the pain and woe
From this I must release my soul

If this illusion is my way
This is the price that I must pay
For all illusion can reveal
Is what exists not what I feel

Beliefs are what they wish to be
And answers come when eyes can see
My heart does fear you will close down
I fear you will not be around

Shadows of this fear have torn
The shroud of pain that I have worn
Desperation clouds my view
When my heart reaches out to you

Should I remain to change my mind
Prove to all my word is blind
Should I face the fears I make
Succeed or fail in this mistake

Shall I give in to my remorse
Change my mind or change my course
Hide myself from what I've done
Or face the self I call someone

Confusion is rewarding me
Blending thoughts with no reprieve
Branding stillness on my heart
With burning pain in every spark

I am not sure of what I'll find
Where myself was left behind
Whether chains will cease to be
On this road to search for me

* * * * * * *

May 9 1979

There is so much to say
Yet each time I try to grasp the words
They slip away
A fire is burning within my heart
My body trembles when you are near
At times I'm not really here
I understand the things as said
I ponder what will happen next
And hide my head in this text
I feel deeply about the connection we share
The importance of taking things slow
Is prevalent because I do care so
You can feel my desire to let go
I know because my eyes have said
That I rule my heart with my head
When I know how precious
This move stresses – I'm careful
This poet has shared poems with few
She feels her passion with her pen
Your acknowledgement has been
Appreciated.
I want to take a chance
Overcome my fears of reaching out
Believe the intuitive glance…and not
Self deception, rejection and doubt
Be patient if I hold my thoughts
For they will emerge in poems
Till I feel at ease
You will know my path thus sought

May 12 1979

Listen to the wind…
As it rustles thru the trees
Telling tales both far and wide
Hear the message in the breeze
Allow the tones to float inside
Softly, gently, intuitively descend

Watch the clouds in the sky
As they float amidst the stars
Feel the motion circulate your mind
Reaching to release rational bars
That protects the self and keeps us blind
Of realities that deem to pass us by

Sense the life that dances about
Creating illusions to tempt our dreams
Desires to own that which is shared
And man-kinds belief forever seems
To divide the universe into pairs
To close doors and lock the truth out

Children of the heavens and of the earth
Existing as is the result of birth
Open your eyes and look again
The world can be different – when?
When you realize what is said by the wind
By the motion of clouds – ere akin
To the life that performs for all to see
There is more than one reality

Listen to the wind; watch the clouds in the sky
Sense the life that dances about
Don't let these worlds pass you by

May 12 1979

Children of paradise
Heaven descended
Lodge in games
Realized yet pretended
Growing in concepts
Wishing for age
Unlimited recess
Of pleasure & rage

* * * * * * *

Untitled

Lay your heart in hand
Send love; life if you can
A puppy is in the crack between worlds
And the choice rests upon him to cure
God if ever I come to understand
Why pain must settle him
He's given us a view of purity
Never will I part from beloved yogi
An angel to the first degree
May the white light set him free

Rachel

June 5

Lady of my heart
Words could never share
The depth in part
And the love you bear
This world knows not
Your songs, your views
Such wisdom sought
By a lady of blues
Open your eyes
Look into the skies
A cosmos reigns of lullabies
At your beck and call
A breath of life
Does leave your lips
Observing your strife
Rise above such dips
Child of paradise
Ripple in a pond
Eyes that glisten with surprise
Wave your music wand
Shower folk with passion
Harmonize with wind
Let intuition control your ration...ale
Ah lady you are a god send

Poetry could never be
A path to express your beauty
Just a window a vision of purity
'Tis poetry

Untitled

Pass the time as wished in word
Sitting positioned amidst the décor
Silent charisma this time is absurd
The note left a mark in appearance of more
Pacing the home you've settled with folk
Leaving to travel: reasons you feel
Important in time… why say I sulk
My heartfelt impressions reflect the surreal
I know not the reason you say what you do
Unsure of revealing these thoughts as they grow
'Long distance run around' seems so true
Perhaps your evasion explains what I know

* * * * * * *

Need I say much more in rhyme?
My poetry cuts through the physical line
Souls in relation have met this time
But this revelation is far from divine
Prophets have knowledge – much to share
Often such knowledge makes them assume
But lessons are learned best when compared
You've yet to experience this karma in bloom
…that which will open your spirit soon
In a manner this reading could never touch tune

First love

Mid summer 1978

Standards have set the rules of relations
Placing some boundaries, few but intense
Though I have tried to avoid complications
I must remain true to the heart of my sense
Often I've said that the man of my dreams
Must be older, wiser with softness of heart
A lover of nature, of musical streams
Of poems and prayers and of me in part
My list can continue for miles of ink
Lists such as this cant be completed
To find a being that conquers each link
Would give me a task that could leave me defeated
I've found a man that fulfills most my needs
I've omitted some rules…here and there
The more time we spend, the little he feeds
Has left me unsure as to how much we share
Now I am pondering rules again
Doubt in my mind has left me a septic
Should I reflect on my contact with men?
Or try next time to be more selective

Cheryl's Lament

February 26 1982

Love has lost its meaning
Fear has come to stay
Pain has closed our friendship
I lost a friend this day

Jealousy has entered
This home in disarray
Mothering has lost its worth
A price we both shall pay

Respect is earned not asked for
Pride has closed your mind
Patience runs away from us
For now your love is blind

Wisdom has departed
Freedom hides from view
Love is nor your weapon
The war is inside you

Sincerity has a shadow
The mirror shields your face
Run and hide behind closed doors
Our love you can't replace

Sisterhood has died young
We buried her last night
You've locked her soul within you
The key is lost in fright

All the words you threaten
Return to share your pain
To use our love in pity
Has left your world with rain

Now love has lost its meaning
And fear has come to stay
Your pain has closed our friendship
You've lost a friend this way

May 12

It takes a little bit of faith
Yes a little bit of love for yourself
When you're lettin' go of him
But you wanna give in
Grab a hold of your will
Just remember it still
Takes a little bit of faith
Yes a little bit of love for yourself
When he's tearin' out your heart
Even though you're both apart
Sayin' works his only friend
That is why our love should end
Before he finds that little faith
Yes that little bit of love
Keep the distance in view
Or he'll take away from you
That little bit of faith
And the love that you feel
For yourself

Untitled

Shadow boxing through the night
A ring of darkness shielding light
Gloves held high defending face
Protecting bruises held in place

A bell has rung to pause the match
Opposing corners set to patch
What wounds appear beneath the skin
To damper hopes of giving in

A sounding of the bell occurs
One emerges one defers
Both would call the match to end
But each debates his part therein

Shadow boxers heads held high
Who's to gain if neither try?
For one alone cannot contest
A thought alone is laid to rest

Shadow boxing through the night
Overwhelmed in senseless plight

Untitled

They say that hearts can meet as one
When lovers find their mates
I've also heard time heals all wounds
No matter whose mistakes

Such words of wisdom fail to speak
Of matters as they are
And thoughts of comfort barely reach
Beyond the rising star

Be still my heart I know you ache
For all that's said and done
The truth of which you clearly feel
Will find a time to come

For when the heart and mind do meet
They both respond as one

Untitled

Somewhere in time I fashioned a choice
How I would handle love offered to me
My decision was formed with help of a voice
That arose from patterns unconsciously

The voice was a charmer
So gracious in heart
And whenever I wandered
It tore me apart
One side would query
The other negate
When my heart became leery
The voice said "Too Late!"
"Too late for the changes"
"You feel you must make"
"You've sworn an allegiance"
"For intolerance' sake"
"You've promised to listen"
"To follow my rule"
"I've healed the incisions"
"The cuts deep and cruel"
"I've released the pain"
"And soothed the tears"
"What more would you gain"
"By not facing your fears"
The voice was a charmer
So gracious in heart
But I knew I must wander
And make a new start

Untitled thoughts
Spring of 1978

In circular motion, a vortex of change
Immersed in emotive response, in style
Opposed to status; imprisoned exchange
Searching for stations to rest awhile.

I'm in love so I say (and cry with a grin)
Cheshire sweet silence withholding my views
Emphatic release of natural sin…
Unaware vanity contacts the blues

Think not I stay for personal gain
Nor cherish the boldness I seek to explore
I try to conceal what appears plain
And quietly cure my hunger for more.

December 22

It's nearing Christmas but there won't be snow
School is at ease, to wit, to vacation
Visit with loved ones far round the globe
Or enjoy the company of self fed elation
What ever is chosen and done in the future
Is entirely and solely up to each person
Destined to changes round the time of the New Year
Amidst the enchanted days to come
No matter the path decidedly chosen
It is meaningless to others surrounding your home
Whether or not the happiest moments
Were alongside pathways of future winds blown

* * * * * * * *

Untitled

Sometimes I find it hard to say
The words that speak my mind
Emotions often try to play
The scenes of every bind
But times I see my heart alone
In pain and agony
It seems to be just like a stone
Inert beneath a tree
I'd like to tell you how I feel
How much you mean to me
Yet 'Neath these thoughts concealed I see
The hurt from every scene
I am as constant as a star
Amidst the blackened sky
The distance traveled is too far
To sit alone and cry

Untitled

Love is the touching of souls
The uniting of two dreams
Containing roads forked with goals
And oddities in streams
If you were liqueur stead of man
I'd drink a case of you
Probably find myself in strands
Cause your proofs too strong in new
But drink I would and not be full
No matter how long in time
For I've found you have a charming pull
That keeps me in this prime

Cherished Songs of our youth

June 9 1979
Poem for Yetta
Written on a night in the presence of a full moon

The sadness comes thru every note
In songs we love so well
Our attitudes seem fit to quote
By those who sing our tale
Yet memories rest in our hearts
Recapturing our past
Though we see only views in part
We see through tainted glass
How hard it is for us to find
The friends we left far behind
But time must pass us uncontrolled
For precious moments must unfold
And new days come for us to share
The richness life and new friends bear
Think not of past and wear a frown
All sweet tunes that reminisce
Should lighten thoughts not bring you down
Magical children, sing in bliss
The present is a pleasant score
And life a treasure chest
Of future memories which we store
In songs of youth all rest

Allen

May 1 1979

A poet I am
And 'ere will be
'Tis in your eyes
I wish to see
Your visions of travel

My body reacts
To the wisdom, the love
And beckons your voice
Reach the clouds up above
Your sun lightened touch

Speak not to a child
The dreamer declares
For her senses in spirit
Do wishfully share
Your desires to live

Belief does beguile
A moment to pass
A moment this child
Wills to peace should it last
Your company, your thoughts

As you follow your heart
Reflect upon verse
The beauty of those
Who are quenched of their thirst
Your existence, your music

December 24 1978

It's the day before Christmas and all thru this house
Boston is playing and I'm getting soused
The cats are up to their usual play
And it seems like a rather common day
There's no sign of mail, nor a ring to be heard
Frankly it's been quite a long time deferred
Santa is dead and won't be arriving
But that won't stop me from surviving
If signs were prevalent in the holy days
Perhaps by morrow I too will praise
But it's mildly warm for Christmas this year
Beautifully shining to bring forth jeer
Many prayers shall reign the skies
But mine are amongst the lullabies
Although this year is soon to close
Existing strings of hope are exposed
The warmest of greetings, kindest of eyes
My thoughts emerge in loving surprise
Carried on wings of whisper winds
I send my heart to all my friends

Lime light rhyme in time

In joy I share, through love I sense
Commonplace in ordered pairs
Thinly veiled…minds seek chance
Seen in dreams of cloudy airs
Be neither past nor future thought
Here and now is all that is
Emphasize what yield is sought
Recall thy treasure chest: sweet bliss
For all you are is there to see
Look inside bring out the light
Death is life like Water Sea
And you so choose to cease the fight

* * * * * * * *

Postscript

New tides form the crescent waves
Of morrows yet to pass
Forsaken all is not, alas
A [new] moon shall rise from eastern skies
Sing lullabies, draw you to sleep
Eternity in dreams so deep
Deemed to leave your conscious mind
Appearances shall mystify
Tears of darkness that you cry
Apart from one so loved afar
Prayers are said in chorus line
As you depart in lime light rhyme

Untitled

Like the fool, I too am traveling on a path
What awareness exists is carelessly considered
Though the precipice is steep the aftermath
Like a dream fading from view, withers

As the magician merits strength and intellect
Holding a scepter upon the elements source
So am I a being with the will to select
That which I determine as my course

The memories flood my vision as reflection
Of causality to which our thoughts are trained
The High Priestess guides the science of detection
For the mind regards belief reasonably feigned

When Mother Nature comes to harbour change
Growth is spread as life projects the force
I greet the Empress humbly in her range
As icy thought is melting from the source

"What of power and of its direction?"
The Emperor asks stiffly from his throne
A thought without an act has no connection
And guidance cannot function all alone

Let inner spirit find the source of being
The Hierophant will answer from above
For all is not in what we are achieving
Perhaps the answer is the self with love

Temptation throws its needy arms around me
A choice of love must come to answer yearning
The lovers whisper softly let it be
For love of mate comes not before self learning

A triumph is upon the dual carriage
Wisdom shielded by the cloak atop
The chariot has reigned a formal marriage
Deciding where to go and when to stop

Untitled

Tell me your name, the country I'm in
Whose leaves change their colors
As soft as the wind
Whose god of the north blows cold in the air
Why am I here and here is where?
Speak to me softly of love in first touch
Of softness and warmth I long for so much
Show me the way to the fold of your arms
Dazzle my brilliance with all of your charms
Lead me to answers I ask in the night
Color the sky with your northern light
And your name you said once again I ask
Is it one whose vibrations are destined to last?
Will you cover my mind with the fall of your snow?
Chill my blood quickly before I will know
Why I'm here?

* * * * * * *

Wisdom Once Removed

Gather the light that shines through the door.
Forget what you've got til you're ready for more.
Rembrandt painted for mankind to see,
The beauty of vision, of reality.

Perceiving the world with reduction in senses
Results in a view of subliminal essence.
By Urizen who wishes to see only face,
Ignoring the truth, closes eyes and turns backs.

Cease this struggle between both spheres.
For sides of the brain have predestined careers.
Together, such knowledge gained by the two,
Can help you discover the self that is you.

LOOKING BACK...

April 3 1987

Looking back to days of youth
I wonder if we see the same
When reminiscing for the truth
To understand the things we blame

How we see the past events
As mirrored in our heart
Reviewing that which compliments
Dismissing faults we cart

Are clouds we see that blue in tint
Faces young without the hint of age
We turn the page of our beliefs
Forgiving just to sense relief has passed
In the travels of our mind
Through a self made looking glass we pretend

Reliving dreams that dare come true
Envision sparks without a flame
The wonderment creates a view
Grand in size despite the gain

Did we really weigh those words
Hear the answer, flash a smile
Were our motions that absurd?
Or just a retrospective wile

Untitled

Is the sun that bright in hue?
Tempers mild, voices light
Another page rewritten too
Overlooking what we might
Along the travels of our life
Through a self made crystal path we pretend

Hypnosis of a special kind
Delighting in the roads we seek
Molding what we call the mind
Preaching strength where we are weak

Is the past divulged in time?
As history, augmented facts
Through memories distilled like wine
Despite precision which it lacks

Can forgiveness take its place?
Shelter yet not hides the storm
Allow us room, to grant us face
Appreciative that time has worn
On the travels of our heart
Through a self made mirror we pretend

Looking back to days of youth
I know we see the game
When reminiscing for the truth
Avoiding things we blame

September 14 1979

The arc in web doth bear the wind
And water's surface doth rescind
The dance of trees
The rustling leaves
Bequeath a simple tale to send
The sails that bear the colored sun
Turn round amidst the wind blown run
To drift away
In bright array
Of depths below [the naked one]
Shimmer light as you return
To parts of earth for which you yearn
And man shall rise
To meet your eyes
Begin a day with much to learn
Perhaps the wind has more to tell
For much is stored within the shell
Hear not the breeze
Nor fair the tease
Of scents the wind doth let you smell

For windy days in thought do dwell
And whisper poet's wishes well

October 26 1979

The media man doth peacefully sleep
And the poet writes beneath his feet
A canine friend beside the bed
Rests with scarf wrapped round his head
A voice bequeaths for silent time
Telling of her noise in rhyme
Media man how you declare
This choice of date by which you share
What poet thinks of your response
Doth mirror selfish needs, so haunts
The wonder poet seeks to know
Doth poet play a role perhaps to show
That trust need not become a part
Of this relay perchance of heart
Yes media man you have control
But slighted glimpse of poet's soul
For she knows not what you beseech
Extent of touch within your reach
Depart at will with eyelids closed
This thought in rhyme is thus composed

Moods

Actions tell as words cannot
The mind as it turns in thought
Scanning, for a medium
Expression can, though harm is done
Watchful as the faces turn
Understanding, as we learn

When to say what you feel
Answering in truth as real
Why is it that people fear
Moods of sadness and of tear
Questioning when one is down
As if it's wrong to cast a frown

Naming moods without due cause
Reasoning is filled with flaws
Turning windward when accused
That silent privilege is abused
Feeling hurt when unaware
Why moods are given little care

Knowing moods cannot be wrong
Except when answers are prolonged
Loved ones ask what they should say?
Nothing....but to go away.

Untitled

Rocking horse of days gone by
Let me ride upon your wood
Tug the reigns and gently sigh
The dreams we understood

Rocking horse remember when
I touched the saddle bare
Searched your mind for answers then
Your voice was always there

Rocking horse do you still see
The girl who loved you so
We'd ride away and never be
Within the world we know

Rocking horse with crystal eyes
Do you live in a home
Listen to a child's cries
Comfort and condone

Rocking horse will you roam free
If children turn away
Will days we shared in fantasy
Immortalize your neigh

Rocking horse of days gone by
I'll always ride your wood
I'll tug the reigns and gently sigh
Dreams we understood

Rocking horse you now roam free
Though children turn away
You live amidst my fantasy
In dreams I hear your neigh

The Spell

Circles yield power
Stars give light
Humans bear hours
Birds treasure flight

Emotion; sensation
Passion; despair
Belief; revelation
Compassion; to share

Squares are stable
With words or thought
To support those unable
To balance the lot

* * * * * * *

February 1

I missed you once again
This time over pool I claimed to be the fool
Who fell in love back then
I felt the sparks within
As though we were along the shore once more
Fallen beneath a whim
I failed to cry
I can't bring on the tears for fear
Of what I now realize
Our love has begun to fade
In the mind that shun thoughts of such kind
As cool as sand in the shade
Perhaps I'll change
When I see you in May on that distant day
And your presence is not so strange
But here's my gift to you till then
I hope you see me through and I too
Will be ready to try and win

July 22

Free verse in bondage
Where can I turn
I bear my cross with heart
Forever thoughts do yearn
Freedom placate my ear
Freeze that which doth bear the wound
Temptation beckons strength I fear
Rising sun marks the twilight moon

* * * * * * *

July 24

He sees through me
He feels my heart
How can he view me
When we are apart

He scares the love I know
He beckons me to reveal
How can I help but show
Feelings quite so real

Clare

We speak alike to one we know; and of response beget
The effort, guidance dost bestow; the silence of regret
Our thoughts delight to grow; of sights unpassed as yet
What comes of love we show; must come of deep respect
We are meant to conquer, the essence of our dreams
As you pledge your heart, how clear your vision seems
And soon to follow suit, the past whose heart redeems
The path his son does travel, the mode of which he gleams
He speaks to us so clearly; we let some thoughts pass by
With cognitive consistency, the meanings we belie
We stand behind our feelings, and he is left to try
And in his silence we do question; for the reason why
Separate desires that wish to speak his mind
Gaze into the image of which our love can bind
And listen to the words we speak, the moods we leave behind
Demanding the attention, of which he is entwined
These thoughts have grown within and share with them I will
For they are meant to share, emotions I do feel
The blessings I bestow of which this poem reveals
Are cast upon thy union with whom the month conceals

Untitled

I wish the wind could carry me to you
I'd only stay a while; just to see your face
And to hear your laugh
Would content my days
I wish the sun could warm my heart
The way you do when you hold me close
To feel the purr of my heart as it races to yours
Would content my days
I wish the clouds could speak my heart
And light the sky above your door; just talking
'bout the days gone by or as they are from time to time
To see an answer light my sky,
To read your thoughts and hear the news
Would content my days
I wish the moon could light the auras
We've expressed thus far, and shine the tremors
We have felt in each and every star; and if this world
Is one of few we've passed these lives
I wish to god whatever will come will continuously
Content our days

January 16

If in creating my world I wanted to see
The purity of love in its simplest forms
I'd form a couple in need of a child
Blossomed creatively philosophy & prose
Gentle as wind as thought can create
United growing from without from within
Like the silence of energy thoughts transpire
I'd form this reality based on desire – will
My thoughts have awakened; actualization
I understand more but there's more to know
Continuous questioning always pervade
The matters that engage in conscious reality

* * * * * * * *

January 24

"And it stoned me just like going home"
With a smile nearly as bright as the sun
To picture the avenue I walked alone
Or to see the full moon gracing the heavens
Could bring the tears to my eyes
Making me once again realize
My euphoria with life

The Ineffable

Not a sound is heard though a voice in there
The eyes do not beckon an answer to share
Though thoughts do travel from mind to mind
Barriers are standing, intonations less kind
Had there been an answer how could we know?
The discussion was empty, the feelings were low.

* * * * * * * *

Untitled

Music maker improvise your tunes with love
Neglect the notes that hold you back
And be attentive to the melodies heard on track
Play the songs you love by Brown
Or those by John
And quietly sing along
You've drawn a crowd to gather round
Perhaps it's time for you to come
Upon the world of which you're from
Hold those keys beneath your palm
And I shall listen in til dawn
Accompany you if you please
Just to feel your presence on the board
Is really all I need, no more

December 19

New tides form the crescent waves
Of a tomorrow that has yet to pass
Alas all is not forsaken
A new moon shall rise from the eastern sky
And sing a lullaby to draw you to sleep
To float an eternity of time through your dreams
Though it seems to leave your conscious mind
Appearances amidst a flame shall mystify
The tears you cry alone in the dark
Apart from one you love afar

* * * * * * * *

Untitled

Jazzman plays a song so sweet
As I arise upon my feet
I'll dance for your return
A melody we've yet to learn

* * * * * * * *

Untitled

You can live without a man, much like a career
But you'll be bored with life with no one to share
One is satisfiable but neither deniable alone
So if given a choice for one or the other pick the latter
For what you accomplish while living matters
But bargain your way to achieving the former
Cause without a man to this life you are a foreigner
And regeneration's impossible to perform alone
Besides even if the two collide can't they atone

February 6

In the second month the day of six
A young man shed his blood
For a reason far too great the cost
For the grounds on which they stood
Strangled by fear he flew through the glass
Was taken by panic as he fled from the scene
On a path up the stairwell to our floor
And above til he finally collapsed
And off he was taken to mend his wounds
With a crowd gathered round in horror and awe
Surprised by the arm of the law and
Of his ill fortune

* * * * * * *

Untitled

Today high on a cloud neath a star
I gaze through the heavens blown by the wind
Sunshine in life how near how far
Blazen heart valentine kindness shall render
Help hours bronze lost in gold
I surrender unfold me as you like
There'll be no competition for love held within
Content to flow 'round flower so fine I'm yours
But you're not mine unless you want to be....free

96

Untitled

I'm having quite a time trying to write
But I know the words that need to be said
After all that was expressed last night
I won't feel at ease til I clear my head
Never before have I loved one as much
Nor given myself in all manners of being
Intensified feelings are released by your touch
Followed by smiles content in their greeting
If I had my choice I'd keep you with me
Though I know that you have to go
My fear is concerned with what is foreseen
But I know that the present has time yet to grow
Believe me when I say that I'll make it alright
When you no longer walk through my door
My effort will shine the days with light
And the nights with a cold shimmering core
Neglect the questions I ask about love
Your answers are felt from within
Just hold me and kiss me beyond & above
And I'll continue loving you as I have been

* * * * * * * *

Untitled

Crying eyes that dwell in pain
Who is left for you to blame?
Lying eyes that swell in shame
Who's to question if you're sane?
Dying eyes that run from hope
Who's the actress in your soap?
Blinding eyes that have no scope
Where's the switch the light you grope?
Childish eyes can you not grow
When do actions stop this show?
Feeble eyes that have no glow
Who will lose the games you know?

97

Untitled

The chains bind my thoughts
Though words find their match
Fetters hold their meanings back
From the life they want to live
Then whatever sparked the lines
Finds no wood to keep it lit
Light that could have stayed aglow
Dims the passages of pen

* * * * * * *

Untitled

Poems, prayer, remarks I feel
Have lost their cage
Though bars still stand
The ink in freer
Than the hand

* * * * * * *

Untitled

Let me love you with my
Dreams of actions I
Would not display
Except in the pillow
Of my mind to the
Touch of your skin

Untitled

Who am I? What do I know?
I know my name, my date of birth
The facts and figures learned in school
The skills and trades to earn my pay
Do these things teach me self worth?
To value time I've spent this way?

Have I searched through every mind?
Compared religion's godly traits?
Philosophers with varied thought
Societies in cultured shame
Do these paths lead me astray?
Or yield the answers I have sought.

My value as a human soul
Is weighed by actions, by deed
What I offer life this time
I mirror by each moments breath
The games learned are based on greed
I strive to know the road I climb

Who am I? What do I know?
I know I have a voice to share
I offer wisdom from my well
The rules I'm learning are my own
With poems I write my feelings bare
To understand our self made hell

Untitled

Promises come easily
As words not actions do
Disappointment freely
Reigns above the pride in you
Who can take the pain away
When you create the cage
For every key that's lost inside
Adds death to days of rage
So how can death of feelings
Relieve the angry scars
When feelings must come screaming through
To bring down all the bars
Then keys once lost need not be found
For bars no longer stand
The chance again to reach your strength
Is placed within your hand
Promises come once again
To greet the tower pride
Disappointment cannot enter
Doors left open wide
If actions are not visible
The words will fade away
Then pain has lost its maker
And you have gained this day

January 7

It's been a day alright well fed on events
Though diligently I followed my clues with care
And was tested for what is 'natural sense'
Followed by emotions; presence prepare: I was there
The men of science: Kametz, Schmidt, Broad
Human in every sense of the word
Not a flinch or trace in the least of fraud
Gathered to study, contribute to worlds thought 'absurd'
The power of the self is of extraordinary force
Earth is the creation of the selves united
Reality is beliefs, emotion, will, of course
And life is the greatest fantasy enacted
What treasures we hold within the subconscious
Endless possible; probable existence for all
God is indeed holy – for we talk of our selves
The beauty of harmony, concealed by our call
And to think we've known it all along!!!

* * * * * * * *

Emotive past time

Cleanse your mind child of day
Await the dreams of lesser years
Twin tissued doll, immobile in flight
Often its changes persuaded by him.

Crafty devil…enjoy delights of play
Yearn not for desires that usher in tears
Perception by day doth differ from night
As do meanings from lines within this hymn.

Full moon in a haze in Texas
Nearing summer of 1978

Texas I really don't know you well
Living these years from within I've lost touch
Trying to recapture the reason for such
Were the angels too civilized, was I afraid
In wanting a slow life to ponder my dreams
Reaching for clouds I've lost land it seems
The guidance I seek is given away
To all who notice my vanity
And my moods that alter so radically
There is no one involved but the self I presume
Interactions are modest, misused by greed
No apologies calm the tensions I feed
The damned are left to search all alone
Pride be their courier, agony their weight
The two intermixed results in self hate
The seeker bewilders the essence of face
Philosophical style conquers in truth
But to practice to die denies one of youth
Parapsychology science of age
Testing the real from the make believe
Though powers as such might very well be
Given the choice to live or to die
A question that rests the bottom of souls
Left to deciders who feel themselves bold
Look at me Texas tell me your thoughts
Do I run from cities, myself and from you
And pretend it's worth all the loneliness too?

The departure

May 2 1979

Go away...
See the places you want to see
Be the man you wish to be
Even if you must leave me

Go away...
Sail seas of dreamers here and now
Follow every whim you vow
Live your life as you know how

Go away...
Keep your thoughts of love inside
Know the self that dwells in pride
Leave your arms open wide

Go away...
Whether you will come again
We'll not know if so til then
Remember I am here, your friend

Go away...
Learn of all that is to pass
Allow your love for me to cast
The light upon your heart of glass

Go away…

Should you decide to come one day
I shall not pressure you to stay
Nor curse the dreams that came your way

Yesterday…today…go your way…

June 25

Words negate the feelings so real
Charm not emotions that passed a blur
Such strength in such weakness
Force from within
A fantasy come true I was sure
Perhaps fleeting moments, romance as such
Percussionist tender to eyes and touch
Suavely appealing to women in all
Brown belted artist move with finesse
Childish eyes of sin
Quietly viewing this woman as such
I wandered in mind from his face
Flattered he viewed me with ease
Deep rooted notions flowed
Guidance for his soul
Tis hard to tell if pure of tease
Will he write and think of me
Has this dream come to end
Gilded tension patiently waits
If only an event, the past
I'm satisfied; I'll make amends

Nightbyrd

Why did you leave? I wonder
Was it something I said? You saunter
Away without saying a word, how else can I say 'it's absurd'
You know not how I felt or thought, why judge me on the spot
My pride asks, yes demands your reasoned reprimands

Why did you leave? I ask
Were not our conversations vast?
Did we not view each other well
Or did we lack an honest tale
I wonder if in my neglect was lost some sense of your respect

Why did you leave? I sigh
Was that your way to say good-bye?
Was my reaction to your being absent of acknowledged feeling
Am I wrong to question you or does it matter – to pursue
In answer to your active deed perhaps I'll know to future heed

Why did you leave? I feel
As if my high was too surreal and you take pride to not reveal......yourself.

Twin answers

Ere I seek the past again tis not my choice my friend
Ere I carry grudges too tis not my thoughts of you
Ere I cry my heart til bare tis not because I do not care
Ere I throw my temper round tis meant such words not be found

Perhaps I wonder if you know
If you care my feelings show
That I have found a place we share
Though truthfully I know not where

Ere I dream to rule your mind tis not with thoughts sent unkind
Ere I ask that you take hold tis meant for you to walk arms fold
Ere I beg to know your soul tis past beliefs I share – a goal
Ere I leave to be alone tis not the essence I condone

If I beseech thee with my eyes
Pass well beyond impulsive lies
Chains shant bind the feelings thus
Tis meant to grow – respect for us

Not as it is – as you pretend it to be – you're trapped

Quiet like shadows dripping with dew
Soft lighted meadows calling for you
Are you trapped in cities walking with dead
Are games that you play trapped inside your head

Hard felt promises follow your trail
Blind years of love doomed you to fail
Are you trapped in cities, match rich against poor
Do games that you play leave you wanting for more

Lost mindless people stand in your way
Self possessed citizens born every day
Are you trapped in cities where life races past
Are games that you play, played til the last?

Cold man made structures threaten the sky
The privileged few take all of the pie
Are you trapped in cities where standards set rules
Are games that you play still ordered in schools

Pollution and ward have come to our lives
Living like robots just to survive
Are you trapped in cities burdened with pain
Are games that you play the games that you blame

Different directions you're lost in the maze
Swearing the earth is the cause of your ways
Are you trapped in cities, run scared and blind
Are games that you play controlling your mind

Chorus:

Hour by hour, day by day
Living tomorrow just minutes away
Pride in your status, your Disneyland
As life passes by the way that you planned

Untitled

I live my life in a dying breed
That tries to distinguish want from need
Tries to find love through conditional threats
And fails knowing both sides will face their debts
My crying won't gather a heart ripped in two
I can't share the truth with emotional glue
Because tact comes apart when the bleeding begins
And I can't live my life counting losses and wins
The struggle continues to hold onto health
Fighting the shame that takes hold of myself
I struggle to see past the parts of the whole
Fighting denial of pain in my soul
My father will hurt me to force in a choice
My mother will back him by cue of his voice
My sister will stand there to see what I do
And my husband will bank on my guts to come through
What will I do when I see the door slam?
Will I destroy all the person I am?
Will guts come to surface when I feel my pain?
Will I join dying breeds if my heart goes insane?
I only know that I'm destined to lose
I'm destined to die or to live if I choose
I'm destined to face all my cultural dues
And my love for myself to this bomb is the fuse

Untitled

A poet walked along the shore, thought did reign her mind
The waves a crest the sands implore a lime light rhyme in kind
Beseeched the skies did beckon winds to scatter sands afar
And seagulls flew amidst the clouds in search of Aslan's star

The sun grew weary of the day and slowly set to rest
As folk along the beach withdrew from reach of water's crest
The poet sat upon the sands beside a castle bare
Searching for the past beliefs her present image shares

The sun did set and moon did rise before the poet rose
Beneath the twilight universe created, she, her prose
And as she turned to walk away from where the castle stood
Her eyes did meet a wooden door that led her midst the wood

The poet walked around the trees who greeted her surprise
For where 'ere she turned the beauty shone like mirrors in her eyes
Nymphs and centaurs roamed the land with dwarfs and fauna dear
And all who chanced to pass her way did greet her loud and clear

The poet knew not where she was nor how this came to be
She knew not if this was a dream nor if reality
Though she did ponder thoughts as such in mindful reverie
A waterfall performed a dance to satyr's melody

Hippy hollow

July 8 1979

Freedom show no mercy…
In the hills of hollow pleasure
On this rocky road I journey
Mark the swimmers naked treasure

Shimmer water in the sun
Shallow depths discard the wind
Wave a crest and then please run
Cast your shadow round the bend

Passion tent in careful form
Sails of silence fair thee well
Pause in life…again reborn
Voice the echo of a shell

Our Life In Death

October 26 1979
You speak of worth in talk of death,
But who doth measure words of breath?
The waste, you sense, we see when gone,
Is not contrived to be condoned.
Perhaps the image in your mind,
Is stimulus of other kinds?
That you have viewed amidst the days
And thoughts like these leave you amazed.
The disrespect we show to corpses
Mirrors our neglect of forces.
We are born to know desires,
Causing senses to admire
Bodies with the soul entrapped,
Awareness which we do not lack.
Ere meant to rediscover such
Without desiring mortal touch.
Ethics of the medic's field
Are shields by which the doctors heal.
Beliefs that paved this practice's worth
Had died in merit since their birth.
Levels of the tension here
As read through novels we hold dear.
Speak not to us to know their cores,
For we do live within their pores.
And when we die and lose our worth,
We will know then to not want birth.
For measures we have judged these by,
Are seen reversed of how they lie.
Acquire all you contemplate.
Society need not relate.
The mode by which you view death pure,
Will put to ease your mind for sure.

Untitled

Quietness silently proud something that cannot be heard aloud

Seldom found amidst a crowd the society of words

Often feelings lose the grace when given a translation

How can it be otherwise – to hold a conversation

<u>Impulse</u> forces ties and labels <u>used by all</u>

To calculate what has to be <u>becoming's lost by call</u>

Child of garden blades of being voice amidst a void

Windless cries sunlight signs shadow less of joy

Carry tunes that dramatize a play of worldly order

Melodies of consequence limit distance border

Silence shuffles quiet quakes keeping touch of time

But can you tell me what is said beneath the poem's rhyme?

M.M.O'Hair

An atheist seeks proof from those who claim
God exists because the burden of proof
Rests upon those who make claims of anything.

An agnostic has no knowledge of a concept
And again the burden of proof rests upon those
Who claim to have knowledge an agnostic lacks.

A scientist seeks to understand that which is
Mysterious.

An artist seeks to express his understanding of
That which is mysterious.

Religion takes that which is mysterious and
Attributes its existence to God.
Why?

Out of fear of discovering that God was (is)
A cover to hide behind when the path to truth
Lay before 'the believer'. The path being more
Difficult to follow than an invisible idol –

Religion leads people, like sheep, away from
Questioning the reality before them.

People prefer to have answers from power
-power that gives them no choice but to
Follow and accept what is given.

To search for answers does not mean one
Is lost; but rather that one has found
The courage to accept the right to
Challenge truth's given by power.

Power does not give truth the right to stand
Apart from question.

Power implies the acknowledgement that
The truth presented is in need of question.

January 3 1978

I wish the wind would carry me away where ever
Through the clouds I can ponder for miles
The moments may pass for eternity t'wouldn't matter
Twin confession lie to others the truth of pain-hidden by smiles

Pursuit of goals long ago desires
May carry the wind in harmony
Though only negligence has transpired
In time patience restores the peace

I've waited for months alone and in fear
Tomorrow's hope kindled by firelight
Through poetry I speak the heart of prayer
Upon forces unknowing I'm asking for sight

Temptation has knocked on my door at all hours
Trying every which means to lead me astray
And faithfully kindled I uncover my powers
To shield me from harm of predator for prey

And the days continue passing in motion
I gather my strength to rise with the sun
Though my life has unfolded shades of emotion
They rest secure united as one

And the pursuit of goals long ago desired
May carry the wind in harmony
Though only negligence has transpired
In time patience restores the peace

A Prayer of 'Song"

December 22

There's a lady out there that needs a hand
She's been crying for years – no one understands
And buried beneath tears is a heart so bare
God please try to find the time to care
Take away the fears that plague her pride
She really needs you there by her side
Ill departed as many do speak
She's only a babe, her harm is quite weak
Can't you find the mercy to guide her away
From the vulgar world she's destined to stay
Sealed in our bodies awaiting the thrust
In the core of our hearts we live by your trust
And you are the source by many we swear
Ablaze in the search to see if you're there
But when needed most where do you lie
No one shall know but with trust we get by
And in you God we trust the prayers of our heart
Hoping in essence that death will not part
The bond as eternal as miracles of few
May it please you Lord we're listening too
Amen

January 21 1996

Mom can you hear me? I miss you so much.
I miss your responses – the feel of your touch
I wish you could sit here and smile again
In so many ways you were always my friend.

Mom can you see me? Reach out for my hand.
Your comfort and guidance are needed again.
I long for a moment to hear your advice
Yet, our time has been taken at such a high price.

Mom can you feel me? I'm scared to go on.
You've always been present, so honest and strong.
I thought we'd share many more years in our lives
But despite prayers and efforts the cancer survived

Mom can you watch me? – protect me from harm
You cared for me well and I feel so disarmed
The emptiness hovers, my heart is in pain
I need you to hold me and kiss me again

Momma I love you with all of my heart
I know that in spirit we won't be apart
When I reach out for answers I'm left holding air
Mom can you help me? Mom are you there?

In Memory of Shirley Ladin
1-21-96

120